Anxiety Relief
COLORING BOOK
FOR ADULTS

This book belongs to

....

About this book

Coloring books have become increasingly popular as a tool to help reduce anxiety and promote relaxation. The act of coloring can provide a meditative and calming experience that can help ease feelings of stress and anxiety.

When you color, you engage in a repetitive and rhythmic activity that can help quiet the mind and focus your attention on the present moment. This can help break the cycle of anxious thoughts and provide a sense of control and accomplishment.

Anxiety Relief Coloring Book For Adults: Calm Your Mind And Enjoy Your Own Meditative Moments is a comprehensive resource that offers an effective approach to help you manage anxiety and stress. This coloring book is specially designed to provide a relaxing and meditative activity that can calm your mind and promote mindfulness.

This book features beautiful and intricate designs that range from simple shapes to more detailed illustrations, allowing you to choose the level of complexity that best suits your needs. As you focus on the act of coloring, you'll enter a state of flow that will help you forget your worries and concerns.

I highly recommend using colored pencils to bring these pages to life. Colored pencils provide a more controlled and precise coloring experience, allowing you to create beautiful and intricate designs that can be both relaxing and satisfying.

If you have a few minutes, we invite you to write an honest review of the book. Your feedback will help us improve future editions and ensure that we continue to create fun and engaging coloring books for adults.

To leave a review, simply visit the book's page on the website that you brought it. We appreciate your support and look forward to hearing from you!

Thank you!

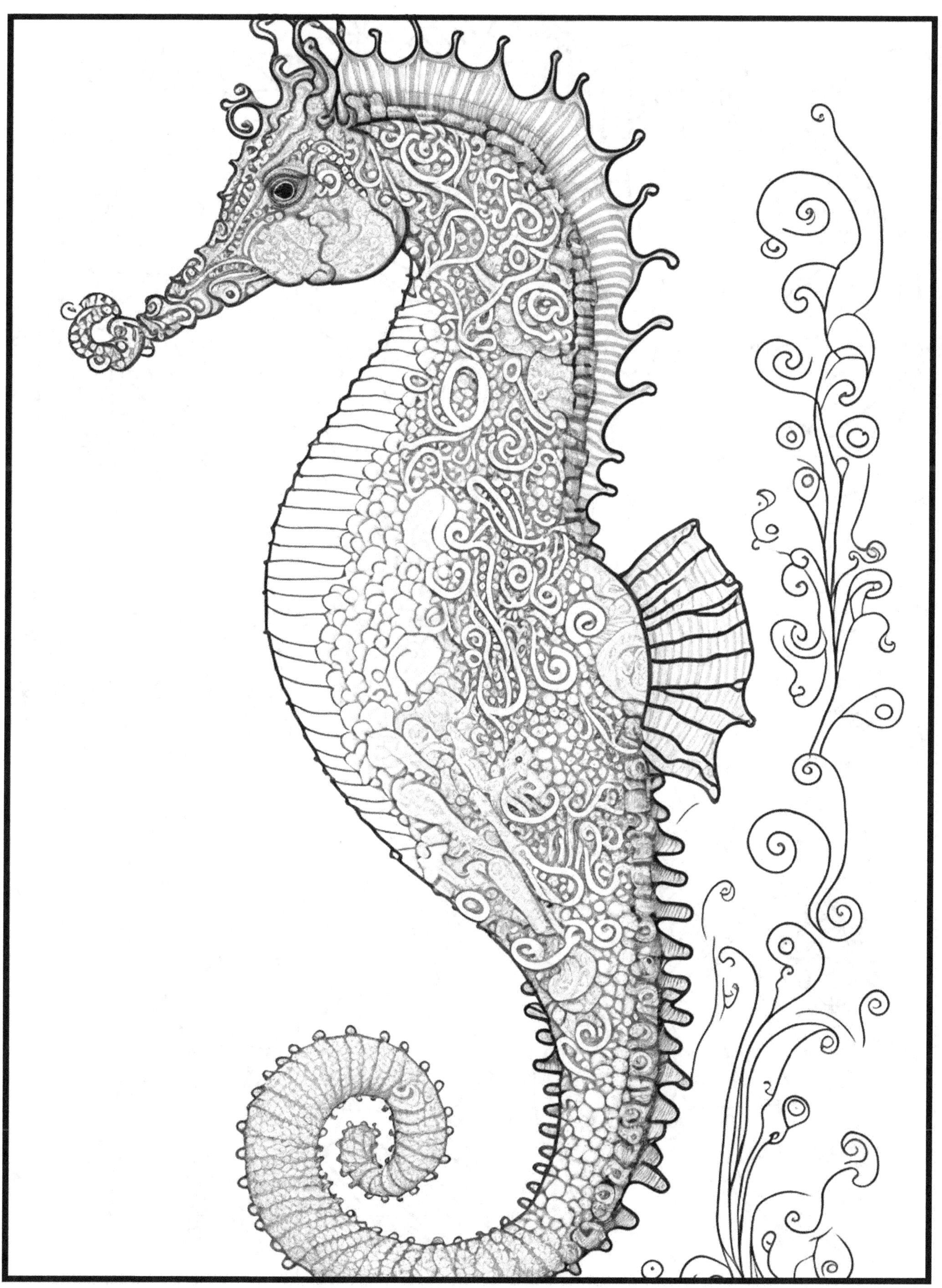

www.ingramcontent.com/pod-product-compliance
Lightning Source LLC
Chambersburg PA
CBHW081439250726
48662CB00009B/2858